Our Journey AFTER DEATH

Human Speculation or Divine Revelation?

W.C. Dietrich

DISPENSATIONAL
PUBLISHING HOUSE, INC.

Copyright © 2019 W. C. Dietrich
Cover: Leonardo Costa

All rights reserved. No part of this publication may be reproduced, stored in a retrieval system, or transmitted in any way by any means, electronic, mechanical, photocopy, recording, or otherwise, without the prior permission of the copyright owner, except as provided by USA copyright law.

"Scripture taken from the New King James Version.
Copyright © 1979, 1980, 1982 by Thomas Nelson, Inc.
Used by permission. All rights reserved."

Printed in the United States of America

First Edition, First Printing, 2019

ISBN: 978-1-945774-30-0

Dispensational Publishing House, Inc.
PO Box 3181
Taos, NM 87571

www.dispensationalpublishing.com

This is a DPH Quick Print book. Our QuickPrint process allows us to get books to the market at a much quicker pace and lower cost than the full book publishing process. If you discover errors in this book, please contact the publisher so that these errors may be fully removed in future editions.

Ordering Information:
Quantity sales. Special discounts are available on quantity purchases by churches, associations, and others. For details, contact the publisher at the address above.

Orders by U.S. trade bookstores and wholesalers. Please contact the publisher:
Tel: (844) 321-4202

Dedicated to my beloved wife
Sandra Crowder Dietrich

June 25, 1946 – June 12, 2016

Table of Contents

Foreword.. 1

Chapter 1: From Death to Afterlife 3

Chapter 2: The Spiritual Realm 11

Chapter 3: Limitations.. 19

Chapter 4: Resurrection, Judgment, and the End Times...... 27

Chapter 5: The Tribulation and The Kingdom of Heaven 37

Chapter 6: The Rest of the Story 45

Chapter 7: Unanswered Questions 51

Chapter 8: My Journey 61

FOREWORD

During our 50 years of marriage, my late wife often said to me, "Bill, you really need to write a book." She knew I loved to write and she thought I had a talent for it. But for some reason, I could never decide what kind of book to write; consequently, I never did. My writing was typically limited to various business communications, letters, and opinion articles. After finally deciding to write this book, I quickly found the task more difficult than I had expected. Because of this, I needed a strong sense of purpose and commitment to remain steadfast.

When my beloved wife died suddenly in June 2016, my grief was understandably painful and continues to this day. My only comfort came from the belief that her precious soul was in heaven where I would someday join her. As a Christian, this is what I had always heard and believed; however, I wanted to see if the Bible confirmed what I had been taught. Knowing that scriptural misinterpretations often stem from wishful thinking rather than from lack of understanding, my direction became clear. I had to write a book about life after death, according to what the Bible actually says. I hoped that my search for the truth would bear the kind of fruit that would satisfy my need to know, as well as that of those who will read what I have found.

Having made the decision to write the book, I first sought counsel from my dear friend and pastor, Dr. Randy White. My wife and I had become friends with him and his family in Katy, Texas where he pastored our church. When he moved to a much smaller church in Taos, New Mexico, we continued to follow his teaching online and continued our friendship as well. One of the benefits of his relocation was the time and freedom it gave him to write and produce more Bible study material. In fact, he founded his own publishing company, Dispensational Publishing House (dispensational-publishing.com), which is the publisher of this book. When I told him of my desire to write such a book, he was not only encouraging but also committed to editing, publishing, and marketing my work. This gave me the confidence to proceed on a journey that has been enlightening, challenging, and somewhat arduous at times. I have told friends and family that if I were writing a book based on anything other than God's Word, I could probably complete it in a couple of months, not a couple of years. Although I thought I knew the Bible fairly well, my eyes were opened through more intensive searching and allowing Scripture to interpret itself. Continuing to benefit from Dr. White's teaching and Bible study methodology has been invaluable throughout this process. I kept in mind that if I am claiming to represent what Scripture actually says, as much as possible I had better make sure I get it right.

I have to admit that not every question we may have about life after death has a crystal-clear answer in God's Word and that some answers may not be found in a single verse or passage. However, I hope to have been careful to document those truths which appear very solid and to acknowledge areas in which different interpretations exist. My hope is that readers will be able to take comfort in what I have studied and that they will find it interesting, encouraging, and engaging to the end.

FROM DEATH TO AFTERLIFE

What Happens When We Die?

It's the question everyone asks throughout much of their lives: "What happens when we die?" Every civilization from ancient times through the present day has believed in some sort of afterlife. Even though there have always been individuals who choose to deny that there is life after death, the majority of people have believed that there is. There have been numerous popular books and movies that claim to be accounts of a person experiencing death and then returning to describe the afterlife. This affirms that there is an apparently insatiable desire to know the answer to this question. Although such accounts may be interesting and entertaining, they lack credible evidence. Many of these accounts have rightly been discredited; therefore, the search for the true answer continues.

The various ways in which a person answers this question are based on an individual's philosophy. If placed on a spectrum, the answers would range from atheism and agnosticism to Eastern mysticism to New Age spiritualism and finally, to Christianity, Judaism and Islam. Because we live in a postmodern era, the popular culture insists that that there is no such thing as absolute truth. In this view, each person can choose his own version of truth and different versions are presumably equivalent. The notion that there is only one source of truth is disputed and ridiculed by postmodernists. Denying absolute truth gives postmodernists confidence that an individual's answer to the question of life after death is a personal matter. However, opposition to their position is simply unacceptable.

Some choose the atheistic answer that denies any sort of afterlife. Therefore, they live with the conviction, and probably the hope, that there is nothing beyond the grave. This philosophy allows one to live life trusting that there is no spiritual component to human beings. As such, there can be no judgment by some transcendent god. There are even those who claim to be Christians who believe that when we die we are annihilated, thus denying any afterlife. Agnostics, being unconvinced of the existence of God, may attempt to live a life that they hope will be pleasing to God – just in case there really is one.

Others embrace various concepts of a spiritual afterlife. A superintending deity or power that has sovereignty over the spiritual and physical realms may be part of this belief system. Every theological philosophy has put forth its ideas on this vital question, yet many people remain unclear about what to believe. Since these ideas vary widely and are in conflict with one another, it should be obvious that they cannot all be correct, even though postmodernism attempts to claim that they are. This conflict exists primarily because all but one of these philosophies are man-made. Such philosophies represent the imaginations of men and can be molded and even blended by the individual to meet his or her emotional and intellectual preferences. As with most decisions in life, our choices often come down to believing what we *want* to believe. By believing what we want to believe, we are simply adopting an answer that most appeals to us and provides some level of confidence and inner peace.

Finding the True Answer

Since there is no universally accepted belief regarding the afterlife, or absence thereof, is it possible that there is one true answer that we can discover? There are two possible pathways to discover what one accepts as truth. One path relies on human theories and emotions, and the other is based on divine revelation from the one true God. Human theories are subject to change, whereas divine revelation is unchanging. A person's beliefs regarding the afterlife and the authority of the Bible as a divinely inspired text have profound and eternal implications. Consequently, it's not a question of what one believes, since a belief in itself will have no effect on reality. No matter how fervently someone believes something, beliefs cannot possibly have any effect on absolute truth. This is because man cannot create truth; he can only discover it.

If there were a means of finding the real truth, would anyone really want to know? For very personal reasons, I want to find the answer from a reliable source. I trust that there are many other people who share this desire. Wanting to know the truth goes beyond our normal sense of curiosity. Knowing whether we will be reunited with departed spouses, family members and other loved ones is one of the primary reasons people want to find the answer. However, there are numerous other questions about the afterlife that send people searching for more answers. If we believe in a creator God, will we be able to see Him and dwell in His presence? Will the afterlife experience be the same for everyone, or will there be marked differences based on how a person has lived his life? Will we have physical bodies? If so, what will we look like and what will be the future of those bodies? Clearly, if the afterlife is a reality, there are a host of questions for which we would want answers. Obviously, we would first ask the fundamental question of whether there is anything which continues to exist after one dies.

In our search for the truth about life after death, we must first ask if there is really only one reliable source of information. The Bible is uniquely authoritative because it has been shown to be self-proving and lives up to its claim to be the inspired Word of God. No other book demonstrates the fulfillment of prophecies in minute detail that were made over thousands of years nor is there any other book whose prophesies are in the process of being fulfilled even now. Whether or not you believe that the Bible is truly inspired by God, it is important to see that there really is no viable alternative. By rejecting the Bible as the most reliable source of the true answer, you are left with purely human speculation. As a Christian, I trust the Bible as reliable and authoritative and have undertaken an extensive study into what it really tells us about what happens after death. I have found that it is not as simple as most of us have come to believe. Unfortunately, even though the truth is to be found in the Bible, there is no individual book or section within Scripture that traces the aftermath of human death from beginning to end. Yet mankind strives to learn as much as God has revealed because, as Ecclesiastes 3:11(NKJV) tells us, God "has made everything beautiful in its time. Also He has put eternity in their hearts, except that no one can find out the work that God does from beginning to end." For this reason, I have engaged in a thorough search for every passage that sheds light on the subject which will enable us to construct the most credible picture possible.

The Physical and Spiritual Realms

We need to determine initially whether there is anything that remains after the body perishes. A belief in a supernatural God who cannot be seen by human eyes is, by definition, a fundamental belief in a supernatural spiritual realm. Clearly, this realm must exist in order for any theological beliefs in a transcendent "higher power" to have a basis in fact. If there is no reality beyond the visible, physical realm, then the concept of the existence of a supernatural God is meaningless and the possibility of life beyond death becomes irrelevant. Communicating with God through prayer also assumes that although unseen, God hears these prayers whether spoken or silent. Furthermore, the concept of salvation must necessarily relate to some aspect of the individual other than the physical body, since everyone eventually suffers physical death. If there is nothing remaining after death, no one would be in need of salvation. Without the existence of a supernatural realm, all of these concepts equate to nothing.

The word "soul" is commonly used to describe the component of every human which exists within us and survives after physical death. This implies that there is a spiritual, non-physical nature that we all possess which embodies our true personage. Our true "self" is not our physical body but rather it is our "soul." Genesis 2:7 describes how God breathed the breath of life into Adam and he became a living soul (*nephesh* in Hebrew). New Testament Greek employs the word *psuche*, from which we derive the English word psyche, to describe this spiritual entity. The soul is the invisible personage that lives on earth and it continues to exist after death. The word "soul" appears more than 500 times in the Bible. Those references confirm that it is our soul living within us that defines who we are. It may be easier for us to visualize the soul as a physical entity existing in the physical domain, but it is essential to distinguish between our physical and spiritual bodies.

There are numerous passages in scripture that support the existence of a spiritual soul after death. Genesis 35:18 refers to the soul of Rachel, Jacob's wife, departing from her when she died. Another example appears in 2 Samuel 12 when King David was fasting because the son born from his treacherous affair with Bathsheba was very ill. When he was informed that the child had died, David ended his fast and said, "While the child was yet alive, I fasted and wept: for I said, Who can tell whether God will be gracious to me, that the child may live? But now he is dead, wherefore should I fast? Can I bring him back again? I shall go to him, but he shall not return to me" (verses 22-23).

David understood that although his son's body had died, his soul now dwelled in a realm where David's soul would also go after his own physical death. In this way, David would be reunited with his son.

Jesus gave powerful evidence to the thief on the cross beside Him of the soul's separation from the body at death. The thief acknowledged that he deserved to be put to death, but that Jesus had done nothing wrong. He then said, "Lord, remember me when thou comest into thy kingdom. And Jesus said unto him, Verily, I say unto thee, Today shalt thou be with me in paradise" (Luke 23:42-43). There was no doubt that both were about to suffer physical death and that their bodies were destined for the grave. However, it was their souls which would be separated from their bodies and move into the realm that Jesus referred to as paradise.

Jesus also gave clear evidence of the spirit's survival after death when He uttered His last words on the cross: "and having cried with a loud voice, Jesus said, `Father, to Thy hands I commit my spirit;' and these things having said, he breathed forth the spirit" (Luke 23:46, Young's Literal Translation). He gave up the spirit of His physical body to the Father, yet His soul and spirit clearly did not perish. He surrendered the breath of life but not His soul. Upon His resurrection, His spirit and soul were returned to His resurrected, glorified body.

Since the soul is a non-physical entity, there is a tendency to use the terms "soul" and "spirit" interchangeably. However, according to both Old and New Testament texts, they are not the same. The Greek word for "soul" is *psuche* and the Hebrew word is *nephesh*, as previously mentioned. The "spirit" is not the soul, but rather the breath of life. The Greek word is *pneuma* and the Hebrew word is *ruach*. In both cases, we see the concept of the spirit related to the movement of air, such as in the wind and in breathing. The soul is the seat of our emotions, desires, and will. Because our soul is our unique essence, we possess self-consciousness. The spirit, however, is that which enables us to have the consciousness of our creator

God and the ability to communicate with Him. When God fashioned the first human, Adam, He breathed the breath of life into him.

At the Last Supper on the night before His crucifixion, Jesus spoke at length about His departure from this earth. Jesus reassured His disciples, saying, "In my Father's house are many mansions: if it were not so, I would have told you. I go to prepare a place for you. And if I go and prepare a place for you, I will come again, and receive you unto myself; that where I am, there ye may be also" (John 14:2-3). Jesus, knowing of His imminent crucifixion, was clearly not talking about building a physical structure and returning to bring His disciples there to live with Him. He did, in fact, return in His glorified physical body soon after rising from the dead and spend time with the disciples. However, He did not take them with Him to a new dwelling place to live with Him at that time. All of the disciples eventually died, and Jesus had not returned to receive any of them in their physical living bodies. There is no scriptural account of Jesus returning to gather His disciples and carry them away.

So was Jesus intentionally deceiving His disciples, or was He talking about returning to receive them in their resurrected bodies at some future time when they would dwell thereafter in the house of God the Father? When we compare this promise to Paul's revelation of the Rapture in 1 Thessalonians 4:13-17, it seems that this could be what Jesus is talking about. On the other hand, it is possible that they will not be raised until Jesus's Second Coming and the establishment of His earthly kingdom. Jesus continued to reassure His disciples and prepare them for His death on the cross, promising, "I will not leave you comfortless: I will come to you. Yet a little while, and the world seeth me no more, but ye see me: because I live, ye shall live also. At that day ye shall know that I am in my Father, and ye in me, and I in you" (John 14:18-20). This is a glimpse into the spiritual realm that neither they nor we can fully comprehend because of the limitations of our physical minds and senses. Yet it does lend credence to the spiritual nature of the soul which transcends the physical body and that resurrection will happen in the future.

THE SPIRITUAL REALM

Heaven, Hell and Paradise

A commonly held Christian belief is that at death the soul of a believer goes immediately to heaven and that of an unbeliever goes immediately to hell. Although there are verses in the Bible that are often quoted in support of this view, I wanted to determine whether there is ample evidence in the original text that either confirms or contradicts this belief. For example, when Jesus said to the thief next to Him on the cross, "today shalt thou be with me in paradise" (Luke 23:43), was He referring to heaven? And when the apostle Paul said that he wished to be absent from the body and present with the Lord (2 Cor. 5:8), does that also indicate that the immediate destination of the soul is definitely heaven? Whatever the answer, we must also consider whether there are any good indications that those not destined for heaven go immediately to hell.

The Hebrew word for "paradise," *pardec*, is only found three times in the Old Testament (King James Version). In one verse it is translated as "forest" (Neh. 2:8), and the other two are translated as "orchard" (Eccles. 2:5 and Song of Solomon 4:13). Other versions literally translate the word as "park." The word for "heaven" appears more than 200 times in Scripture, and in all cases, it is literally translated to mean "sky or skies" in both Hebrew and Greek. Generally, the sky can be defined as everything outside of the confines of the earth. In Genesis 1:1, God created "the heavens" (*hashamaim*) and the earth. This is the same Hebrew word that is used throughout the Old Testament and it always refers to the region above and beyond the earth. The sky is mentioned as the abode of birds as well as the home of God. There is no other word which is specifically used to describe the place where souls of the departed go to be in God's presence. In New Testament Greek, there is also a single word (*ouranos*) which is always used to mean heaven in the same way it is used in the Old Testament. Since Jesus instead used the word "paradise" rather than "heaven" (Luke 23:43), this suggests that perhaps He was referring to a more specific place than the general place and that the word "paradise" may not be interchangeable with heaven. He could have said, "Today you will be with me in heaven," but instead, He used the word "paradise." The Greek text actually includes the definite article "the" in all three verses in which paradise is mentioned. Therefore, we should not assume that paradise and heaven are necessarily synonymous.

Jesus refers to "heaven" numerous times in the New Testament:

- Matthew 5:34 "…heaven… is God's throne";
- Matthew 6:10 "…Thy will be done in earth, as it is in heaven";
- Matthew 6:20 "…but lay up for yourselves treasures in heaven";
- Matthew 6:26 "…yet your heavenly Father feedeth them."

There are many more references to heaven as the dwelling place of God. However, that does not confirm the belief that souls of the departed proceed immediately to heaven.

In 2 Corinthians 12:2-4, Paul relates a vision he received from the Lord in which he seems to equate the "third heaven" to paradise:

"I knew a man in Christ above fourteen years ago, (whether in the body, I cannot tell; or whether out of the body, I cannot tell: God knoweth;) such as one caught up to the third heaven. And I knew such a man, (whether in the body, or out of the body, I cannot tell: God knoweth;) How that he was caught up into paradise, and heard unspeakable words, which it is not lawful for a man to utter."

Furthermore, in Revelation 2:7, John also refers to Paradise: "To him that overcometh, will I give to eat of the tree of life, which is in the midst of the paradise of God." Since the Old Testament translation of the word paradise is "forest" and "orchard," it could also be interpreted as "garden." And because the tree of life, which we know from Genesis 2:9 is in the Garden of Eden, it is conceivable that paradise is actually the heavenly restoration of the Garden of Eden. However, if paradise is the place which we define as "heaven," why is the word "paradise" not consistently used in other contexts which seem to refer to the eternal dwelling place of saved souls?

Next, there are 54 verses (31 in the Old Testament and 23 in the New Testament) in the King James Version of Scripture that contain the word "hell." None of these verses should be taken to indicate a direct pathway from death to the final place of everlasting torment. To explore the idea of "hell," one must seek out a literal translation of the original Hebrew and Greek texts. The most authoritative literal translation I have found is Young's Literal Translation of both Old and New Testaments. Young's translates the Hebrew and Greek texts literally but never translates the words *Sheol* or *Hades*. Yet the King James and modern translations almost always translate these words as "hell." Actually, Sheol is simply the place of the dead. Likewise, Young's does not translate the Greek *Hades* as hell either, as this was understood to be the same place of the dead as *Sheol* is in the Hebrew language. The Amplified Bible, which is a literal translation in most respects, also does not translate *Sheol* or *Hades*. It simply adds a parenthetical note which says, "region of the dead."

It is interesting to note that the King James translators completely removed the words *Sheol* and *Hades* and translated these words differently based on context. When referring to the death of someone whose death is to be mourned, the KJV translates it as "the grave" or another non-condemning word. In most other cases, however, it is translated as "hell." This exposes such word choices as interpretations rather than translations, since the words cannot have completely different or opposite meanings based on context.

The problem is that the use of the words "heaven" and "hell" as commonly taught are without basis and create misunderstandings which further confuse the issue. The King James Version's introduction of the word "hell" as a substitute for Sheol and Hades was derived from an Old English word of Germanic origin: *hel*. This word means hidden, unseen, concealed, or unperceived. When interlinear texts seek to translate the Hebrew and Greek words *Sheol* and *Hades*, both are typically translated as "unseen." This supports the assumption that the place of the dead is inhabited by disembodied spiritual beings which cannot be seen by human eyes. Unfortunately, the word "hell" has been almost universally transformed in the Christian church and in our popular culture to mean the state of eternal torment. It is a place of punishment for unrepentant sinners and those who reject Jesus as Messiah. The New Testament word which describes the true "hell" as Scripture defines it is possibly *Gehenna*. This likely refers to the lake of fire in the book of Revelation. In short, the use of the word "hell" as a fair translation of *Sheol* and *Hades* represents a serious stumbling block which stands in the way of a full understanding of the pathway from death to eternity and introduces doctrinal conflicts along the way.

Different Sections in Sheol/Hades

Jewish tradition, as reflected in Scripture, held that although Sheol is the place of the dead, the obedient and faithful Jews were said to be destined for "Abraham's bosom." This was a place of comfort and reward for living a life that honored the God of Abraham, Isaac and Jacob, and in subsequent generations, for living in obedience to the law given to Moses. Jesus related an interesting parable to His disciples (Luke 16:19-31) in which He describes two distinct areas in the spiritual realm of the afterlife (Hades) which are separated by a broad, impassable gulf. The rich man who had lived a life of worldly excess descended to an area of flaming distress, whereas the beggar, Lazarus, was in the comfort of Abraham's bosom. The rich man called out in agony and pleaded with Abraham to send Lazarus to dip his finger in water and come cool his tongue. He also asked Abraham to send Lazarus back to his living brothers to warn them that they would end up in torment if they did not repent of their sinful ways. But Abraham answered that the brothers still had Moses and the prophets to warn them of their ways. The rich man responded, "Nay, father Abraham: but if one went unto them from the dead, they will repent." Abraham then replied, "If hear not Moses and the prophets, neither will they be persuaded, though one rose from the dead."

There are those who claim that this parable should not be taken to represent any literal view of the nature of Hades because it is purely allegorical. While it is true that parables use allegory and symbolism to illustrate a moral message, that does not mean that there are no literal aspects to be considered. Jesus did explain to His disciples why He used parables to demonstrate certain truths. Jesus's parables always depicted relatable experiences and events. Jesus used this parable to illustrate a message regarding the eternal consequences of how one chooses to live with respect to God. More significantly, it was prophetic in predicting that many Jews would reject Him even though He would rise from the dead. While this parable would not make sense without calling Abraham by name, it would be unnecessary to call the beggar, Lazarus, by name if the parable were purely allegorical. However, identifying both characters by name tends to support the impression that the parable has both literal and allegorical aspects. Those who focus on various interpretations of the allegorical aspects of this parable offer other reasons for calling Lazarus by name. Yet I believe we should also focus on what this passage may reveal about the real nature of the afterlife. It gives us evidence that even though the characters are representative of people who have died and are presumably spiritual, they are recognizable and able to communicate with each other. It also alludes to limitations and boundaries that exist within the domain of Hades, which is important to remember as we explore the nature of the afterlife.

While heaven and hell may be the final destinations of the departed, there are relevant questions about whether this transition is immediate, as many have been taught. It will also be necessary to sharpen our perceptions about what we describe as heaven and hell. The initial step to a correct understanding requires further exploration of the biblical concepts of Sheol and Hades, as we have already done. In both the Old and New Testaments, it is apparent that Sheol/Hades is the first stop once the soul departs from the body upon death and is the place where the souls of the departed abide. To some, this really makes no difference as long as the end result is essentially correct. However, there are many who want to know, like the late Paul Harvey, "the rest of the story." When you study the totality of biblical references to the afterlife, the notion of immediate passage to heaven or hell stands in contrast to a large body of Scripture. For example, it creates an illogical understanding or negation of the Rapture. It also disregards the roles and dispositions of the departed during the millennial kingdom and eternity future. Furthermore, those who seek to discredit the Bible's validity will try to focus on these instances in which there appear to be conflicts. In subsequent chapters I have more thoroughly demonstrated how conflicts regarding life after death are a result of misunderstanding and misapplication to the appropriate biblical dispensation.

Did Jesus Descend into Hell?

For many years I was troubled by one of the versions of The Apostles' Creed which says that Jesus "was crucified, dead, and buried; he descended into hell; the third day he rose again from the dead." I thought that if hell is indeed the place of torment for unrepentant sinners, why would Jesus have to go there? And how does that not stand in conflict with Jesus's promise to the thief on the cross that "today you will be with Me in Paradise"? Clearly, paradise is not hell as we think of it, but neither is it necessarily heaven.

The idea that Jesus descended into hell seems to come from 1 Peter 3:18-20: "...being put to death in the flesh, but quickened by the Spirit: by which also he went and preached to the spirits in prison, which sometime were disobedient..." Close examination of these verse reveals that there is no mention of hell or Hades. The interpretation that hell is the place where disobedient spirits were imprisoned goes beyond what the Scripture actually says. In fact, the word in the original Greek which is translated as "prison" (*phylake*) would more accurately be translated as "guardhouse." This seems to indicate that these spirits or souls were being kept in confinement awaiting some future event, not that they were necessarily being tormented or punished. The reference to disobedient spirits in the days of Noah may also refer to the fallen angels who rebelled against God along with Satan.

So, why did Jesus "preach" to the souls of the departed? The original Greek text indicates that He "proclaimed" or "heralded" to them. His purpose becomes clear in the following chapter. "For this cause was the gospel preached also to them that are dead, that they might be judged according to men in the flesh, but live according to the will of God" (1 Peter 4:6). It does not seem unreasonable to conclude that Jesus would make known to the souls of those who were already dead in the flesh that He was the long-awaited Messiah.

Eternality of the Soul

The Bible is sufficiently clear that there is indeed a spiritual life of the soul that continues beyond the death of the physical body, and we also know that the soul has the property of eternal existence. In the New Testament, the Greek word for "eternal" (*eonian*) appears more than 70 times. The word most often refers to eternal life, but it is also used to refer to eternal punishment many times. Probably the most widely quoted and recognized verse of Scripture, regardless of whether a person believes or not, is John 3:16, which says, "For God so loved the world, that he gave His only begotten Son, that whosoever believeth in him should not perish, but have everlasting life." This not only affirms the existence of the soul, but it also affirms that this soul will live eternally. The promise of uninterrupted eternal life can only pertain to the soul and not the physical body since every person born will suffer physical death, including those who believe in Jesus. Hebrews 9:27 tells us, "It is appointed unto men once to die, but after this the judgment." Because of the reference to the final judgment of the unsaved in Revelation, we know that this does not happen until after the end of Christ's thousand-year, earthly reign. This is called the Great White Throne judgment, in which the unsaved will be cast into the lake of fire. Saved souls will be judged at an earlier time but will receive rewards rather than condemnation. It is obvious that the phrase "after this" does not necessarily mean immediately afterward, but simply refers to a future event.

In summary, we can say that upon the physical death of the body, the spiritual body travels into the unseen realm of disembodied souls and awaits the next step in the journey toward an eternal destination. For some it will be an exciting pathway filled with hope and reward, while for others it will be a daunting pathway headed towards the ultimate punishment. Thankfully, the Bible has given us enough information to fill in most of the blanks with as much detail as God has chosen to reveal through His Word.

LIMITATIONS

The Seen and Unseen Domains

Scripture makes clear that God and other heavenly beings normally exist in the spiritual realm. This is a domain which human eyes are unable to perceive. Thus, when the soul departs from the body and moves into the unseen domain, it enters into the realm which God also inhabits. However, this is not to be confused with heaven or hell because it is only the first step in the journey. As previously mentioned, interlinear translations of the words *Sheol* and *Hades* are both translated as "unseen" or "unperceived." In effect, these regions of the dead cannot be seen by living people. As physical, created beings we live in a universe that we can only see through our eyes. We can *apprehend* that there is an imperceptible realm, but we cannot actually *comprehend* such a realm. That is to say, we can grasp the concept of an invisible, infinite domain but cannot fully and completely understand it or visualize it in our finite minds.

When we try to explain our understanding of events or beings acting in the invisible realm, we must resort to descriptions which can be visualized in perceptible, earthly terms. There are, however, physical phenomena and forces that we can perceive without actually visualizing them. Air, wind, X-rays, cosmic radiation, heat, sound waves, radio waves and television signals are but a few examples of this. We see their effects, so we know they are real even though our eyes are incapable of directly viewing them. Life would indeed be unbearably confusing and distracting if all invisible phenomena were visible! There would be so much visual "noise" bombarding our eyes that we would be unable to focus on anything.

God's very first creative action is described in Genesis 1:3 when He created light and pronounced that it was good. We often overlook the fact that light as we know it did not appear to exist before God created it! His first creative act stands as the most fundamental cornerstone of His entire creation because without light nothing else could function. Light itself cannot be accurately described by science despite endless attempts to do so. It is well known that light spans a broad spectrum of wavelengths. Only a portion of that spectrum lies within the range that enables our eyes to see. So-called visible light is the invisible medium by which the physical world around us is made visible. Plant life depends on light as the energy source necessary for photosynthesis to occur. Light transmitted from the sun provides the heat necessary to maintain the earth's temperature within the range needed to sustain life. In one way or another, all life on earth depends on this foundational phenomenon we know as light.

Yet God took care to place necessary limits on light in order that it would serve the needs of His created order. By separating light from darkness, which is the absence of light, He created the cycle of "day" and "night" so there is evening and morning. This was the first day of His creation. After creating the atmosphere and separating the dry land from the seas and creating plant life, He then created the sun, moon, and stars on the fourth day. Up until that point, the source of the light was God Himself. He transferred the source of light to the heavenly bodies He created. They would thereafter provide the separation between the day and the night and be used for signs, seasons, days, and years. It is obvious from the beginning of Genesis that order and purpose are fundamental aspects of God's character. In His creative process,

He established separations and boundaries such as light and dark, earth and firmament, dry land and seas. We can only speculate about God's infinite purpose in creating a finite universe, but He clearly established a separation between the finite and the infinite domains. Our finite bodies can neither see the infinite domain nor cross this boundary while we are living beings; however, God created an eternal soul within us which will make this transition after death occurs.

The Timeless Domain

The unseen domain appears to also be a timeless domain, as God is timeless and therefore eternal. In 2 Corinthians 4:18, Paul writes that "the things which are seen are temporal; but the things which are not seen are eternal." Peter echoes this idea, "But, beloved, be not ignorant of this one thing, that one day is with the Lord as a thousand years, and a thousand years as one day" (2 Peter 3:8).

Therefore, we need not be concerned that our departed loved ones may feel a sense of confinement for years or even centuries while awaiting the next step. In fact, the souls of the first Christians have been absent from their physical bodies for almost 2,000 years! Do we really believe that they are aware that this much time has passed since their death? Without the earthly cycle of daylight and darkness, the method by which time is measured is absent. We should therefore be thankful that their souls reside in the timeless domain in which the Lord also resides.

When God created the cycle of light and darkness, He effectively created the concept of time. In the simplest sense, time is the method we use to track the ongoing changes that result from the structure and mechanisms of the universe that God designed. We now understand that the periods of day and night result from the rotation of the earth on its axis. We also know that the earth travels in its orbit around the sun and this journey takes 365 day-and-night cycles, which we call a year. We have divided the year into twelve months consisting of four seasons. Day-and-night cycles have been further divided into hours, minutes, seconds, and ever smaller divisions such as milliseconds, microseconds, and nanoseconds. These increments of time necessarily pertain to the physical domain, which will eventually pass away and be replaced by a new heaven and new earth. When that occurs, there will be no sun to give light and no darkness. As it was before the fourth day of creation, the source of light will be the glory of God Himself.

The universe is a dynamic system, meaning it is in constant motion yet is not fundamentally changing. As a wheel traveling on a road is changing positionally, it is still a wheel. A clock's hands are constantly changing positionally, but the clock is still a clock. So what was God's purpose in creating time? From the beginning, when He created the sun, moon, and stars, He said, "Let there be lights in the firmament of the heaven to divide the day from the night; and let them be for signs, and for seasons, and for days, and years" (Gen. 1:14). We know from Scripture that He is timeless. He is not subject to the constraints of time since He created time itself. Unlike God, man is constrained by time and necessarily views events in terms of past, present and future. God has inspired the recording of historical events and His interactions with His creation since the foundation of the world and has provided knowledge of future events through prophets He has chosen.

Scripture reveals to us that not only is the spiritual domain timeless, but it is also partitioned. We know from Jesus's parable about the rich man and the beggar named Lazarus that there are divisions in the realm which are invisible to the temporal world. Lazarus was in a section of contentment and the rich man was in a section of torment. Likewise, we are told that there are barriers which prevent free movement from one section to the other. Whether we call it Sheol or Hades, Scripture reveals that this is clearly not the final destination. We must look to the book of Revelation to learn what the final destinations of heaven and hell will look like.

The Transition

My search of Scripture strongly indicates that the first stop in the afterlife journey is Hades. However, the popular belief among Christians is that when a believer dies, his or her soul proceeds immediately to heaven. It is also commonly believed that the soul of the unbeliever goes immediately to hell. Interestingly, these contrasting views rely on the same passages of Scripture but are interpreted differently. Paul states in 1 Thessalonians 4:16-17 that those Christ-followers who have died prior to the Rapture will rise first. Those who are still alive at that time will rise to *join together with them* to meet Jesus in the air. The passage beginning in verse 16 says that "the Lord himself shall descend from heaven with a shout, with the voice of the archangel, and with the trump of God: and the dead in Christ shall rise first." It seems obvious here that the souls of the dead in Christ have not yet risen until this very time. It continues in the next verse, "Then we which are alive and remain shall be caught up together with them in the clouds, to meet the Lord in the air: and so shall we ever be with the Lord ." Again, it seems clear that this is a single sequence of events in which the souls of the dead, followed by those living at the time, will join together to meet Jesus in the air and will thereafter be with Him forever.

It is almost universally believed by Christians that the souls of believers proceed immediately to heaven upon death. Indeed, I have not been able to find any notable theologians who strongly disagree with this.

In an effort to support the notion that the soul of the departed goes immediately to heaven, some believers give an alternate explanation of the Rapture. This scenario claims that Jesus will descend and bring the souls of those who have already died and gone to heaven to return and participate in the Rapture. I believe that this idea results from a misinterpretation of 1 Thessalonians 4:14, which says, "For if we believe that Jesus died and rose again, even so them also which sleep in Jesus will God bring with him."

Careful examination of this verse, combined with verse 16, shows that only Jesus descends from heaven and precedes the rising of the souls of the dead. It does not mention Him bringing a massive multitude of souls with Him from heaven. Grammatically, the subject of the last clause of this sentence is God, not Jesus. Furthermore, if we examine the original Greek, we find that God does not bring those who were asleep in Jesus with Him. It is more correctly translated that He (God) shall be *leading them forth together toward Himself*.

As previously mentioned, souls who have departed the physical body initially reside in the unseen realm where God also resides. Jesus called this initial destination paradise, where He and the thief on the cross who believed in Him immediately went upon their respective deaths. Therefore, we can reasonably say that one who is "absent from the body" is also "present with the Lord." If paradise is *actually* an area in Hades, it is clearly not the final destination we call heaven. This is especially obvious since those souls in paradise will rise first in the Rapture and join together with those still living to meet Jesus in the air. Have they gone to heaven, only to turn around later and participate in the Rapture, and then go back to heaven? This seems a little far-fetched, doesn't it? More importantly, nothing in Scripture would support this view.

If the souls of those who were already dead do not actually rise until the Rapture, how could they have been "present with the Lord" since the time of their death? And if they have not been actually in His presence, where have they been? Shouldn't we continue to question whether there is any good evidence that the Christian soul goes to heaven immediately upon death? By relying on the concept expressed by Paul in 2 Corinthians 5:8 (i.e., "absent from the body... present with the Lord"), a significant and erroneous short circuit seems to have been created. This assumption results in misunderstanding and conflict with other writings of Paul. The full context of this passage reveals that while we are at home in our bodies, we are absent from the Lord, and that we would be well pleased to "be absent from the body" and "present with the Lord." Scripture does not define "present with the Lord" as being synonymous with heaven. Neither does this indicate that the transition is immediate. But in an attempt to reconcile this question, some theologians have invented the notion of "soul sleep," which also lacks any basis in Scripture. This represents a common problem that occurs when a verse or a phrase is taken out of context and woven into church doctrine because it is simplistic and sounds good or comforting in certain situations. Yet both the statements in 1 Thessalonians and 2 Corinthians are true and are not in conflict.

The idea that the souls of deceased believers are dwelling in paradise while awaiting the Rapture seems to be the only reasonable explanation. This agrees with 1 Thessalonians and 2 Corinthians and supports the belief that the church will be gathered as one body to proceed to the next step in the journey together. It does not seem consistent with the totality of Scripture to describe the first step in the afterlife journey as heaven because there are several extremely significant events that will have to occur prior to the creation of the new heaven and the new earth to come.

RESURRECTION, JUDGMENT, AND THE END TIMES

The Resurrection of Believers

One point to remember is that Hades will not be eliminated at the Rapture. The only souls to rise from Hades at the Rapture are those who believed and trusted in Jesus as their savior. This is what we know as the Rapture of the church.

At the Rapture, the members of the body of Christ will become united and proceed to heaven with the Lord Jesus. All of those saved souls whose bodies have died will be brought forth out of paradise to join with those believers still living at that time. Scripture tells us that they will all appear before the Judgment Seat of Christ. This is not a judgment for sins but for the deeds and misdeeds of Christians, to whom a reward will be given. "For we must all appear before the judgment seat of Christ; that everyone may receive the things done in his body, according to that he hath done, whether it be good or bad" (2 Cor. 5:10). Because we are saved by His grace through faith, our salvation is not at risk. However, our rewards will be determined by the things we have done while in our earthly bodies.

The Rapture will remove all Christians from the earth, both the living and the departed souls in paradise; therefore, the church age will end. It is clear that the souls of the departed will receive their resurrected bodies, which have been described as glorified bodies. They will no longer be disembodied spiritual souls but will now take part in eternity future having uncorrupted bodies. Then the raptured church, with both the living and resurrected souls, will go to heaven together.

In 1 Corinthians 15:35-54 the apostle Paul gives a detailed explanation of the resurrection of those who have been saved by grace through their faith. This is a wonderfully revealing passage that begins with the question, "But some man will say, How are the dead raised up? and with what body do they come?" Using a similar illustration as Jesus, Paul uses the example of the sowing of a seed and the germination of a new plant to illustrate this process. Some of the key verses in this chapter include:

- 1 Corinthians 15:37 – "And that which thou sowest, thou sowest not that body that shall be, but bare grain…"

- 1 Corinthians 15:44 – "It is sown a natural body; it is raised a spiritual body. There is a natural body, and there is a spiritual body."

- 1 Corinthians 15:51-52 – "Behold, I shew you a mystery; We shall not all sleep, but we shall all be changed, in a moment, in the twinkling of an eye, at the last trump: for the trumpet shall sound, and the dead shall be raised incorruptible, and we shall be changed."

This last verse lends further credence to the idea that the souls of those who have died prior to the Rapture are not already in heaven but are awaiting the trumpet that initiates the resurrection at the Rapture.

Therefore, it appears certain that the Rapture marks the point at which all Christians – both living and dead – will receive their new, incorruptible, glorified bodies. Just as Jesus was resurrected, we who are saved will be resurrected in bodies which may be recognizable, yet possibly different in appearance. Jesus returned to earth for a short time after His ascension and interacted with people in His glorified body. Although He was able to prevent people from recognizing Him, as He did in the passage about the walk to Emmaus (Luke 24:16), we should not assume that we will have such ability. ("But their eyes were holden that they should not know him.") He had the power to appear and disappear at will, as well as the power to enter into a room whose door was locked (John 20:19,26). When Jesus appeared to the disciples, He bore the marks of His crucifixion so that they could confirm that this was indeed the Christ. Even Thomas, who wanted to touch His wounds, was then convinced that He was risen from the dead.

As we look forward into our future in eternity, there are inevitable questions. Who among us has not wondered whether we will be able to recognize our departed loved ones in heaven? What will they look like? Will they look the same as they did at the time of their death or at a different age? How will we find each other among the millions of Christians there? And what about the millions of innocent babies who have been unmercifully slaughtered by abortion? Will they have bodies that they would have had outside of their mothers' wombs? And what about those who died in infancy due to accidents, war, genocide, or disease?

How we wish we could find concrete answers to these questions; however, God has not chosen to provide them definitively through His written Word. Yet we know His nature and character as revealed through Scripture. We can rely on the fact that He is the epitome of justice and mercy. Therefore, we can have complete trust in His wisdom and love for His creation.

The Road to the End Times

It is an understatement to say that there are differing views regarding the end times. While some argue about the timing of the Rapture relative to other end time events, others dispute whether the Rapture will even occur at all. There are many prophesies regarding the Tribulation, the Second Coming of Christ, and the battle of Armageddon. Scripture also describes the millennial kingdom of Christ on earth, the final judgment, the new heaven, the new earth, and the New Jerusalem. These represent elements of the last days which stir debate among theologians and laymen alike. To some, these elements are but pieces of a puzzle which can be arranged in whatever order one chooses, depending one's assumptions about the totality of the Bible and its fundamental principles. Interpreting Scripture in a spiritual sense rather than a literal sense intensifies confusion and controversy. Departing from the literal interpretation opens the door to human theories and chaos.

Although it is not the purpose of this book to stake out a dogmatic position on how these pieces fit together, it is necessary to explain the interpretive grid I use in terms of end times events. As previously stated, I am convinced that Scripture portrays a journey in the afterlife which has a number of stages. It would be far too simplistic to assume that the story ends with good people dying and going to heaven and bad people dying and going to hell. In order to believe that, we would have to disregard biblical prophesies which have been fulfilled as well as those yet to be realized. We would also have to ignore the promises God has made throughout the Old and New Testaments. Unfortunately, there are those who have built their theology without regard to prophesy. Others simply choose to interpret prophesy in a way that is based on what they desire God's Word to mean rather than what it actually says.

Admittedly, there are numerous passages in Scripture which are not intended to be taken literally. In these cases, such as in the parables of Jesus, it is easy to see that they are figurative, not literal accounts. However, the majority of the Bible is comprised of literal accounts of events that do not require spiritualization or interpretation. There are also accounts of prophetic dreams or visions which are identified as such. Sometimes an interpretation of the vision is provided and in other times it becomes necessary to search the Scriptures to arrive at the most plausible meaning. Serious study of the Bible relies on the practice of *letting Scripture interpret Scripture.* One of the many sources of such study material is found in the psalms. While many look upon the book of Psalms as merely poetry, careful study reveals extensive prophesy within the psalms. There are, of course, the 17 books of the Old Testament which are known as the prophetic books, from Isaiah through Malachi. Many prophesies in these books have already been fulfilled yet many remain unfulfilled.

Although prophesy about the end times is found throughout Scripture, there are two books of the Bible which contain perhaps the most detailed information on this subject. The books of Daniel and Revelation provide insights that are both enlightening and challenging in our quest to clearly understand the events that will take place at the last days of the earth as we know it. There have been widely differing opinions over the centuries regarding various interpretations of these books. Much of the controversy has resulted from differences in fundamental assumptions about the historical roles of the Jewish nation and the Christian Church. However, if there is to be clear understanding of what happens in the end, it is essential to understand what happened in the beginning.

After God created the heavens and the earth and then created Adam and Eve, He placed them in the Garden of Eden. The only thing He prohibited them from doing was to eat of the tree of the knowledge of good and evil. Their disobedience to God thrust mankind into a cursed existence of sin and death. But God also promised that the time would come when He would send a redeemer to rescue mankind from the grip of Satan. In Genesis 3:15, the Lord said to Satan: "And I will put enmity between thee and the woman, and between thy seed and her seed; it shall bruise thy head, and thou shalt bruise his heel."

In other words, the offspring of a woman (Jesus) will bruise (crush) the head of the serpent (Satan), and Satan will bruise Jesus's heel. By virtue of Jesus being crucified and rising from the dead, He defeated Satan and would destroy him in the end. While Jesus was suffering on the cross, His feet were nailed to it and He had to try to push upward in order to take a breath, thereby bruising His heel. Suffocation was the actual cause of death by crucifixion, as it became increasingly difficult to straighten up and take a breath. In order to finish this process, the legs of the thieves on the crosses next to Him were broken, thereby preventing them from breathing. They did not have to break Jesus' legs because He was already dead when the guards came to do this. This was another fulfillment of prophesy, as observed by John: "For these things were done, that the scripture should be fulfilled, A bone of him shall not be broken" (John 19:36). The reference here is to Psalm 34:20: "He keepeth all his bones: not one of them is broken."

God's Chosen People

It's no coincidence that the lengthiest portion of the Bible, which we call the Old Testament, was written in the Hebrew language. The overwhelming majority of the text is comprised of the history of God's dealings with the people He set apart as a favored ethnicity – the Hebrews. These are the descendants of Abraham, to whom God made a promise known as the Abrahamic Covenant. When God made this covenant with Abraham, He directed Abraham to go into a land that He would show him (Canaan) and said: "And I will make of thee a great nation, and I will bless thee, and make thy name great; and thou shalt be a blessing: And I will bless them that bless thee, and curse him that curseth thee: and in thee shall all families of the earth be blessed." Not only did God promise to make Abraham the father of a great nation, but would give the land of Israel to these chosen people as an everlasting possession: "For all the land which thou seest, to thee will I give it, and to thy seed for ever" (Gen. 13:15).

Genesis 12 marked the beginning of the biblical history of the Hebrew people, which continued through the rest of the Old and New Testaments. The New Testament book of Matthew begins with the genealogy of Abraham through the 42 generations leading to Jesus Christ (Matt. 1:1-16). God kept His promise to bring His chosen people into the land of Israel and has protected them against many attempts to exterminate them as a unique race. Even though they have been conquered several times throughout history and cast out of the land, God has always provided a way for their return, as He is doing even today. There is ample proof within Scripture and the historical record that references to God's chosen people invariably mean the Jewish people, the descendants of Abraham, Isaac, and Jacob. God actually changed Jacob's name to "Israel," which is the reason the Jews are called the children of Israel. His twelve sons were named as the heads of the twelve tribes to which God gave their respective parcels when they entered into the Promised Land.

Later, when the Jewish people decided that they wanted an earthly king instead of honoring God as their king, God allowed this to happen. God gave Saul as their king to show them the grave consequences of rejecting of Him. God selected David as Saul's successor because David was a man after God's own heart. God subsequently promised that in the end He would set up the kingdom of heaven on earth, and that the King of this future kingdom would be a descendant of King David. Even though the land of Israel would be taken away from the Jews and they would be removed from their homeland, this King would come and restore the land to His people. Even today, Jews await the coming of this "anointed one," the Messiah, who will usher in the messianic age.

According to prophesy, Jesus the Messiah would come and the Jews would reject Him: "He is despised and rejected of men; a man of sorrows, and acquainted with grief: and we hid as it were our faces from him; he was despised, and we esteemed him not" (Isa. 53:3). John witnessed this prophesy being fulfilled and stated: "He came unto his own, and his own received him not" (John 1:11).

When this was fulfilled, Jesus was crucified, and the hopes of the Jewish people were not realized. Even Jesus's resurrection from the dead was not convincing to the Jewish leadership nor to the majority of Jews in general. However, some Jews did believe Jesus was indeed the Messiah and gathered together in assemblies which led to the future Christian church. Initially these assemblies (*ecclesias*) were made up of Jews in various parts of the Mediterranean world. They continued to live as Jews under the law of Moses and were said to be followers of the "Way"(Acts 22:4). They were severely persecuted by the Jewish leaders – the Pharisees – who were determined to eradicate the belief in Jesus as Messiah and to stop the spread of the Way.

As the majority of mainstream Jews continued their rejection of Jesus, the number of Jewish and non-Jewish followers increased dramatically in response to the apostle Paul's missionary efforts. As a Jew, Paul continued to preach to Jews as well as non-Jews, explaining that he had received a revelation from Jesus that salvation was being offered as a gift to all who believed in Him. Paul even had to persuade the leaders of the assembly in Jerusalem, namely Peter and James, that Gentile members of the Way were not to be required to convert to Judaism. Neither should they have to adhere to the law, the requirement of circumcision, nor the multitude of other Jewish regulations. Jews who rejected Jesus continued to live under the law. What began as a Jewish sect ultimately separated from Judaism and it became clear that a new dispensation had begun, known as the age of grace or the church age.

This did not mean that God had withdrawn His covenant with His chosen people, the nation of Israel, nor does it mean that the church has replaced the nation of Israel as God's chosen people, as some in Christendom have come to believe. The continuation of the special relationship with Israel and progress toward the restoration of the Jewish kingdom has simply been put on hold in order that the other nations could be brought into the redemptive plan of God. The church age will continue until the time of the Rapture, after which God will return His focus to His chosen people, the Jews. Understanding this fact is essential in our efforts to comprehend what will take place during the end times. Failure to accept that end-time events are about reconciling the Jewish nation to Himself causes Christians to misinterpret Scripture on many levels.

THE TRIBULATION AND THE KINGDOM OF HEAVEN

After the Rapture

The Rapture marks a fork in the road in the pathway to eternity. With the coming of the Rapture, the age of grace will end and those who were saved by their faith in Jesus Christ will be raised to heaven. Their journey is not over, but they will not have to suffer through the Great Tribulation, which will follow the Rapture. This will be the time when God turns His attention to His chosen people, the Jewish nation. The stage will then be set for the Antichrist's rise to power, the Tribulation, and the Second Coming of Christ.

In the ninth chapter of the book of Daniel, he is given a prophetic vision which provides the key to understanding the Great Tribulation, its timing, and its purpose. Daniel 9:24 states, "Seventy weeks are determined upon thy people and upon thy holy city, to finish the transgression, and to make an end of sins, and to make reconciliation for iniquity, and to bring in everlasting righteousness, and to seal up the vision and prophecy, and to anoint the most Holy." In this context, the term "week" refers to seven years, not days. Thus, 70 weeks equals 490 years (70 x 7).

Of these 70 "weeks," 69 (483 years) are accounted for as follows: seven of these weeks (49 years) were for the release of the exiled Jews from Babylon and the rebuilding of the Temple in Jerusalem. Then there were 62 weeks (434 years) until Jesus came and was crucified ("cut off"), and the Temple was once again destroyed:

> Know therefore and understand, that from the going forth of the commandment to restore and to build Jerusalem unto the Messiah the Prince shall be seven weeks, and threescore and two weeks: the street shall be built again, and the wall, even in troublous times. And after threescore and two weeks [62 weeks] shall Messiah be cut off, but not for himself: and the people of the prince that shall come shall destroy the city and the sanctuary; and the end thereof [shall be] with a flood, and unto the end of the war desolations are determined. (Dan. 9:25-26)

The timeline of this prophesy has been fulfilled, except for the remaining week of seven years. The Messiah did come and was crucified (cut off) and the Romans (the people of the prince) did indeed destroy the Temple and Jerusalem in 70 A.D. Then the Jews were cast out of Israel and dispersed throughout the ancient world. Christianity had already taken hold, first among Jewish believers and then among non-Jews. Many Jews initially believed that Jesus was the Messiah and these believers became known as followers of the Way. These Jewish believers were severely persecuted by the establishment Jewish leaders.

The growth of Christianity throughout the ancient world was largely influenced by the apostle Paul, a Jew who had once been a chief persecutor of those Jews who were believers in the Way. The mystery of grace was revealed to Paul by the risen Jesus himself and he was directed to take this gospel to both Jews and to non-Jews. Through his missionary journeys and letters to the assemblies he ministered to, Paul attempted to persuade the dispersed Jews that Jesus was the Messiah. He also preached to them the doctrine of grace, which previously had not been revealed. Since the time of Moses, Jews had primarily been deemed righteous by living under the law and were resistant to this doctrine of grace which removed them from the requirements of the law.

Gentiles had not been subject to the law, and began to readily embrace the idea that they could be saved to eternal life by their acceptance of the gift of salvation simply by trusting in Jesus as Lord. Therefore, to this day, Christians are living in the church age, or the age of grace. Until the church age is ended with the Rapture, the fulfillment of Daniel's prophesy regarding the remaining week of seven years of God's dealing with the Jews is "on hold." Over time, Judaism and Christianity diverged and the Church became almost entirely made up of non-Jews, or Gentiles, as they are called today. Unfortunately, much of Christendom came to believe that God had abandoned the Jews and that Christians had replaced Israel as God's chosen people. This error has resulted in very troubling misinterpretation of Scripture, and has hindered many from coming to a true understanding of the end times.

The Wrath of God

There are those in the Christian community who either do not believe in the Rapture or believe that it will occur during or after the seven-year period known as the Tribulation. Since Daniel's prophesies exclusively relate to the Jewish people, and specifically to Jerusalem, the focus of the Tribulation is very clear. This is a time of God's wrath being poured out on His chosen people who rejected Jesus as Messiah and a time when Jewish people will come to understand their error. Lest Christians fear or believe that they may have to live through the Tribulation, they can be assured by 1 Thessalonians 5:9-10, which states, "For God hath not appointed us to wrath, but to obtain salvation by our Lord Jesus Christ, Who died for us, that, whether we wake or sleep, we should live together with him."

The wrath of God referred to here is the time of Jacob's Trouble which is also called the Day of the Lord and is found more than 30 times in Scripture, from Isaiah through 2 Peter. It is a great and terrible day which is unlike any other day. Some verses in Scripture give us a glimpse into what this day will be like:

- Isaiah 13:6 – "Howl ye; for the day of the LORD is at hand; it shall come as a destruction from the Almighty.

- Joel 2:31 – "The sun shall be turned into darkness, and the moon into blood, before the great and the terrible day of the LORD come."

- Zephaniah 1:18 – "Neither their silver nor their gold shall be able to deliver them in the day of the LORD'S wrath; but the whole land shall be devoured by the fire of his jealousy: for he shall make even a speedy riddance of all them that dwell in the land."

The book of Revelation records the vision of the end times that was given to the apostle John. The seven-year period preceding the Second Coming of Jesus Christ is the time of the Tribulation, during which the Antichrist will rule. At the mid-point of these seven years the Antichrist will require absolute loyalty to himself and will even claim to be God incarnate. God will allow His wrath toward the nation of Israel to be poured out through the Antichrist, who will unmercifully persecute those who do not bow to him.

This fulfills Daniel's prophesy and causes a separation between those who follow the Antichrist and those who reject him. In Zechariah 12:10, the Lord says:

> And I will pour upon the house of David, and upon the inhabitants of Jerusalem, the spirit of grace and of supplications: and they shall look upon me whom they have pierced, and they shall

mourn for him, as one mourneth for his only son, and shall be in bitterness for him, as one that is in bitterness for his firstborn.

Jewish people who realize that the Antichrist is a false messiah and reject him will be persecuted and some will be martyred. The remaining ones who persevere until the end of the Tribulation will enter into the long-awaited earthly kingdom of God after the Second Coming of Christ. Jesus will return to Jerusalem and defeat its enemies in the campaign referred to as the battle of Armageddon. He will cast the Antichrist and his false prophet into the lake of fire and establish Himself as King. His angel will bind Satan and cast him into the abyss, where he shall remain until the end of the millennium. Jesus's reign will last a thousand years, after which Satan will be released from the abyss for a brief period. Revelation 20:8 says that Satan "shall go out to deceive the nations which are in the four quarters of the earth, Gog and Magog, to gather them together to battle: the number of whom is as the sand of the sea." He will go out into the world to spread deception and recruit a vast army to make war once again against Christ and Jerusalem. God will then intervene and utterly destroy Satan's army. John writes about this in Revelation 20:9, "And they went up on the breadth of the earth, and compassed the camp of the saints about, and the beloved city: and fire came down from God out of heaven, and devoured them."

Jews who have lived righteously according to the law and looked forward to the coming of their Messiah will have already been resurrected at the second coming of Jesus. Those who were martyred during the Tribulation for refusing to accept the mark of the beast will also be resurrected and will serve with Jesus during His thousand-year reign:

> And I saw thrones, and they sat upon them, and judgment was given unto them: and I saw the souls of them that were behead-ed for the witness of Jesus, and for the word of God, and which

had not worshipped the beast, neither his image, neither had received his mark upon their foreheads, or in their hands; and they lived and reigned with Christ a thousand years. (Rev. 20:4)

After this, God will finally cast Satan into the lake of fire where he will be tormented forever. The souls of the unrighteous will then be called forth from Sheol/Hades to face the Great White Throne judgment. When His throne appears, heaven and earth will disappear. Those who have died, except for Christians who were raised in the Rapture, will be brought out of Hades in their resurrected bodies and judged according to their works. In Revelation 20:12, John describes his vision of this when he writes, "And I saw the dead, small and great, stand before God; and the books were opened: and another book was opened, which is [the book] of life: and the dead were judged out of those things which were written in the books, according to their works." Those whose names are not found in the book of life will be cast into the lake of fire. Death and Hades will also be cast into the lake of fire, marking the end of the curse of death (Rev. 20:14-15).

All Things New

The final two chapters of the book of Revelation provide us with the most remarkable description of what eternity will look like. The apostle John was allowed to see the vision of the new heaven and the new earth once the old heaven and earth have passed away. In Revelation 21:5, he describes what he saw: "And he that sat upon the throne said, Behold, I make all things new. And he said unto me, Write: for these words are true and faithful."

The new earth seems to bear little resemblance to the earth as we know it. For example, there is no more sea and no more sun and moon, since the glory of God is once again the source of light (Rev. 21:1,23).

We see the parallel in the creation account in Genesis of God being the source of light before He created the sun, moon, and stars on the fourth day. The new earth likewise bears some similarity to the Garden of Eden before the fall. Adam and Eve blissfully dwelled with the Lord, without the knowledge of good and evil and without death, which is similar to what we read in Revelation 21:4: "And God shall wipe away all tears from their eyes; and there shall be no more death, neither sorrow, nor crying, neither shall there be any more pain: for the former things are passed away."

The centerpiece of this new earth is New Jerusalem, which is revealed to John as it descends from heaven. John refers to the New Jerusalem as the bride of Christ:

> And I John saw the holy city, new Jerusalem, coming down from God out of heaven, prepared as a bride adorned for her husband... And there came unto me one of the seven angels which had the seven vials full of the seven last plagues, and talked with me, saying, Come hither, I will shew thee the bride, the Lamb's wife. And he carried me away in the spirit to a great and high mountain, and shewed me that great city, the holy Jerusalem, descending out of heaven from God... (Revelation 21:2,9-10)

While it is difficult to understand how the city can be the bride of Christ, that is clearly what is stated here. It would not be too much of a stretch to assume that this New Jerusalem represents the Jewish people. This concept is no more difficult to understand than the church being referred to as the bride of Christ, which is an element of replacement theology. The city's fabulous size and beauty are described in intimate detail, including the mention of pure gold, precious stones, gates of pearl and the tree of life, which was also in the Garden of Eden (Rev. 21:18-22; 22:2).

There are many indications that these last days, spoken of from Revelation 19:7 through the end, are all about God's redemption of His chosen nation of Israel. The focus is entirely on Israel, Jerusalem, and the Jewish people. The center of the new earth is the holy city of Jerusalem, which measures 1,500 miles long, wide, and high! It is adorned with inscriptions regarding the twelve tribes of the children of Israel and the twelve Jewish apostles of Jesus. John gives a description of the new Jerusalem in Revelation 21: "And had a wall great and high, [and] had twelve gates, and at the gates twelve angels, and names written thereon, which are [the names] of the twelve tribes of the children of Israel... And the wall of the city had twelve foundations, and in them the names of the twelve apostles of the Lamb" (Rev. 21:12,14).

The description of the holy city, New Jerusalem, is unmistakable in its exclusive connection with the Jewish people and the prophets. One has to wonder, therefore, where are all the Christians who were raised to heaven in the Rapture? Absent any specific information answering this question, are we only left with speculation? Not so fast....

THE REST OF THE STORY

What Happened to the Church?

One of the most prevalent opinions among Christians is that they are Christ's army who accompany Him at the Second Coming. Revelation 19:14 describes this army: "And the armies which were in heaven followed him upon white horses, clothed in fine linen, white and clean."

All we know about Christ's army is that the soldiers are on white horses and are clothed in white and clean fine linen. That does not necessarily connect them with the raptured church. On the contrary, of the more than 100 mentions of fine linen, 88 are found in the Old Testament and mostly pertain to the Jewish priesthood. In all cases, linen is prized clothing. Further, we find that the bride of Christ, which is the New Jerusalem, is to be adorned in fine linen, white and clean. So, what is indicated by this white linen?

Revelation 19:8 brings us to another popular misconception among Christians. The verse says that "the fine linen is the righteousness of saints" (Rev. 19:8). Many believe that "saints" are the church, or the followers of Christ. This is a bit odd, since the word "saints" is consistently a translation of both Hebrew and Greek words meaning "holy ones." The context throughout the Old and New Testaments usually points to faithful Jews as saints rather than to Christian Gentiles. When Christians subscribe to replacement theology, claiming that the church has replaced Israel as God's chosen people, confusion and misinterpretation abound. This is particularly problematic when trying to interpret the book of Revelation.

Although the events described in Revelation pertain almost exclusively to the judgments and redemption of God's chosen race, the Jews, this should not mean that God has forgotten the raptured church. After all, He raised all Christian believers, both living and dead, to be with Him in heaven. And as Paul writes in Galatians, those who are Christ followers are no longer distinguished as Jew or Gentile. He says, "There is neither Jew nor Greek, there is neither bond nor free, there is neither male nor female: for ye are all one in Christ Jesus" (Gal. 3:28).

From the time of Christ until today, few Jewish people have chosen to acknowledge Jesus as their Messiah, Lord, and Savior. Therefore, the separation will continue for the time being. Through the millennium, the emphasis is on the Jewish people. This doesn't necessarily exclude non-Jews from participation in the kingdom; however, the ultimate purpose is the restoration of Israel under the lordship of the descendent of King David.

At some point, prior to the middle of the Tribulation, the Temple will have been rebuilt. We know this because it will be desecrated by the Antichrist. But it becomes clear that there will be no distinction between Jew and Gentile in New Jerusalem. Even though Jerusalem was historically the heart and soul of Israel dating back to the days of King David, in the end all who bow down to Christ are citizens of Jerusalem. This is reinforced by the fact that there is no Jewish temple there, as seen in Revelation 21:22, which states, "And I saw no temple therein: for the Lord God Almighty and the Lamb are the temple of it."

The light of the city comes from God and the Lamb, and this light will shine on all its occupants. This includes Jews as well as non-Jews, who are described as "the nations." The Greek word used here is *ethnos*, which is usually translated as "nations" or "Gentiles," and normally refers neither to Israel nor to the Jews. Although it is not translated as Gentiles in the following passage, one can reasonably conclude that this may be referring primarily to Gentiles but could include both Jews and Gentiles. The mention that these are "saved" would further identify them as believers who had, therefore, been raised in the Rapture and found in the Lamb's book of life. Revelation 21:24-27 states:

> And the nations of them which are saved shall walk in the light of it: and the kings of the earth do bring their glory and honour into it. And the gates of it shall not be shut at all by day: for there shall be no night there. And they shall bring the glory and honour of the nations into it. And there shall in no wise enter into it any thing that defileth, neither whatsoever worketh abomination, or maketh a lie: but they which are written in the Lamb's book of life.

This group could also include those who come to belief in Christ after the Rapture. We know that all Christians, whether living or dead, will be raised in the Rapture. The seven-year Tribulation will follow, but there is no indication how much time may intervene. Although it is said that the church age ends with the Rapture, I find no evidence that God withdraws His offer of salvation to all who call upon His name. Entrance to the kingdom will be made available to those who overcome the Tribulation by rejecting the Antichrist and accepting Jesus as the true Messiah. Furthermore, I believe there is no reason to believe this will only pertain to Jewish people.

Roles in Heaven

As much as Christians seek to ascertain our roles in the end times, there is precious little we can point to in this revelation of Jesus Christ. The central theme is, as it has been throughout most of the Bible, God's choosing of the Hebrew people and the fulfillment of His promises to redeem Israel.

With the completion of the seven-year Tribulation and the establishment of the kingdom of Jesus Christ in Jerusalem, Daniel's prophesy will be fulfilled, which states, "Seventy weeks are determined upon thy people and upon thy holy city, to finish the transgression, and to make an end of sins, and to make reconciliation for iniquity, and to bring in everlasting righteousness, and to seal up the vision and prophecy, and to anoint the most Holy" (Dan. 9:24).

When Jesus Christ establishes His kingdom in Jerusalem, the most holy place, it will last a thousand years. At that time, He will have bound Satan and destroyed his followers in the battle referred to as the battle of Armageddon, so what will be happening during this thousand-year period? Those who have overcome the Tribulation will enter into the kingdom and will have an incredibly peaceful life during this age, free from Satan's deception. Some will be born and some will die because death will not be destroyed until the end of the Millennium. There will be millions living outside of the will of God during this time, many of whom will be recruited by Satan once he is released from bondage at the end of the Millennium. Once this happens and they try to make war on Jesus, they will be destroyed, and Satan will be cast into the lake of fire, as we are told in Revelation 20:9, which states, "And they went up on the breadth of the earth, and compassed the camp of the saints about, and the beloved city: and fire came down from God out of heaven, and devoured them."

With the completion of the Millennium and the remaining end times events, we now seek to discover what life will be like in the new earth and the New Jerusalem. The good news for all those who will dwell there is that the curse of death will be removed forever. Not only will people live forever, but they will also serve God continually. "And there shall be no more curse: but the throne of God and of the Lamb shall be in it; and his servants shall serve him" (Rev. 22:3).

So what does it mean to serve Him in this new earth in our resurrected bodies? We have instructions about how to serve God in our earthly days, don't we? Jewish people try to serve God by living according to the law; however, since the Temple no longer exists, it is impossible to actually live in accordance with the law. Yet their hope is in the promise that they shall live again and enter into the earthly kingdom of God when the messianic age is established. In fact, if you go to Jerusalem and look toward the Old City from the Mount of Olives, you will see a remarkable sight. There are hundreds, perhaps thousands, of graves covering the slopes all the way to the city wall. These are the tombs of religious Jews who want to be first in line to be resurrected when the Messiah comes to usher in the kingdom so that they may enter with Him.

Christians are encouraged to live godly, moral lives and to be ambassadors for Christ, testifying of the gospel of salvation through grace and the substitutionary sacrifice of Jesus Christ as payment for our sins. Without question, we will experience indescribable joy in serving our Lord in whatever way He determines. Many suggest that the rewards we receive at our judgment may define the levels of our positions and responsibilities in the kingdom and thereafter. Scripture does not provide us with this information, but we can be sure that our heavenly lives will be unimaginable!

CHAPTER 7

UNANSWERED QUESTIONS

Missing Some Details

There is either great joy or intense sadness in the knowledge that there is a pathway laid out in Scripture for the both the righteous and the unrighteous. Because we are living in the age of grace, those who have accepted the gift of salvation by believing and trusting in Jesus Christ have secured their eternal home in heaven. Righteousness is credited to the account of every saved person. The good news for those living in unrepentant unrighteousness is that the hopelessness of their current final destination can be exchanged for joy. Romans 10:9 states, "That if thou shalt confess with thy mouth the Lord Jesus, and shalt believe in thine heart that God hath raised him from the dead, thou shalt be saved."

The security that comes with this knowledge should be sufficient for all who are curious about the mystery of salvation in the afterlife. God has not only given us this assurance but has also revealed more than simply the final destination. Through His inspired Word, He has shown us the pathway to that destination. Yet He hasn't given us every detail and has left some facets of the journey for us to explore in His Word. Ecclesiastes 3:11 (NKJV) states, "He has made everything beautiful in its time. Also He has put eternity in their hearts, except that no one can find out the work that God does from beginning to end." We may try to interpret Scripture in ways that go beyond what it actually says or means, and this can easily lead to misinterpretation if we are not careful.

Here are some of the most common questions that may not be fully answered, but thorough Bible study may lead us to reasonably accurate conclusions. We may find passages which appear to answer a given question, but when we get to heaven, we may find out that we completely misunderstood the passage. We may even settle on an answer which provides comfort and peace of mind, knowing that we may be incorrect. But simply believing that something is true does not make it true.

Can the Departed See Us Who Are Still Living Today?

Scripture does not tell us specifically whether or not the departed can see the living, but it seems highly unlikely. We know that God has such power, but let us not presume that we would possess such power. Furthermore, since there will be no sadness, pain, or suffering in the new heaven and the new earth, we need not be concerned nor hopeful that this could be happening now. Revelation 21:4 adds that "the former things are passed away." Anyone who looks at the world we live in today would have to admit that there are plenty of things that are creating sadness, pain, and suffering. Also, being in the literal presence of our Lord will focus their attention on Him and likely shield their spirits from longing to know what is happening in the earthly realm.

What Will We All Look Like?

This is not too difficult if we can assume that the same criteria we find in Scripture will apply to us. We know that when Jesus returned after His resurrection, He was recognizable by those who saw Him. They could touch Him, and He even ate a piece of fish with His disciples. In Luke 24:39-43, He affirmed that His body was indeed flesh and bones:

> Behold my hands and my feet, that it is I myself: handle me, and see; for a spirit hath not flesh and bones, as ye see me have. And when he had thus spoken, he shewed them his hands and his feet. And while they yet believed not for joy, and wondered, he said unto them, Have ye here any meat? And they gave him a piece of a broiled fish, and of an honeycomb. And he took it, and did eat before them.

We know from the appearance of Moses and Elijah on the Mount of Transfiguration that they, like Jesus, were recognizable and able to engage in conversation as well:

> And it came to pass about an eight days after these sayings, he took Peter and John and James, and went up into a mountain to pray. And as he prayed, the fashion of his countenance was altered, and his raiment was white and glistering. And, behold, there talked with him two men, which were Moses and Elias: Who appeared in glory, and spake of his decease which he should accomplish at Jerusalem. (Luke 9:28-31)

Assuming that our resurrection bodies will have these same characteristics, we can expect to be tangible and able to speak and eat. Jesus's glorified body still bore the wounds of His crucifixion, yet He could appear and disappear at will. All we know is that our heavenly bodies will be of a higher order than our earthly bodies and will likely have capabilities far beyond what we now have.

Since a person may die at any stage of life, we wonder whether the resurrected body will appear to be the age at which the person died or some other age. This probably won't matter because the resurrected body will be glorious in appearance regardless of age and physical condition at the time of death. Yet we can't avoid the question regarding the millions of babies and children who died at such an early age. Will we see them, and will they have the adult bodies they would have had? First we need to address whether they will be in heaven or not.

What About the Death of Young Children?

Sadly, millions of children have died since the beginning of time without reaching a level of maturity at which they could know God and Jesus Christ. In the United States alone, over 60 million babies have been crushed and dismembered through the cruel and murderous act of abortion since the 1973 "legalization." Millions have died of illness, accidents, and violent means. Love and compassion drive us to find out whether the souls of these innocents will be saved or allowed to suffer the eternal torment of the ungodly and unsaved. In order to rightly address this issue, we must clarify how people are saved versus eternally condemned.

With regard to mature individuals, we find that apart from the law and the numerous injunctions to follow it, right standing with God has always come through belief and faith in the one true God. Abraham believed and was deemed righteous. This was long before Abraham could even know about Jesus. Genesis 15:6 tells us that Abraham "believed in the LORD; and he counted it to him for righteousness."

After the law was given through Moses, Jewish people were judged righteous based on their obedience to the law, which also provided for annual covering of their sins through atonement. Non-Jews could continue to be found righteous through faith in God apart from Jewish law by believing and trusting God and living a life pleasing to Him, as seen in Romans 1:18-20:

> For the wrath of God is revealed from heaven against all ungodliness and unrighteousness of men, who hold the truth in unrighteousness; Because that which may be known of God is

manifest in them; for God hath shewed it unto them. For the invisible things of him from the creation of the world are clearly seen, being understood by the things that are made, even his eternal power and Godhead; so that they are without excuse…

Although Gentiles had no excuse for not believing in God, they had not been made aware of God's redemptive plan for them until it was revealed. Without expectation of eternal salvation, they lacked specific promises regarding their salvation. As Paul explained in Ephesians 2:12, "That at that time ye were without Christ, being aliens from the commonwealth of Israel, and strangers from the covenants of promise, having no hope, and without God in the world." After the birth, death, and resurrection of Jesus Christ, the gift of salvation by grace was revealed and became effective from that point forward. Paul underscored this in verse 13: "But now in Christ Jesus ye who sometimes were far off are made nigh by the blood of Christ."

Acceptance of this gift relied solely on belief and trust in Christ as Savior. As Jesus declared: "I am the way, and the truth, and the life: no man cometh unto the Father but by me" (John 14:6).

So how does God deal with those who are not intellectually mature enough to comprehend who God is and have neither heard nor believed the gospel of Christ? Although they have not believed what they have not heard or understood, neither have they heard and rejected God and the Gospel. When Scripture does not provide a specific answer to our questions, we must rely on the character of God, which is revealed in many ways. We know Him to be a God of justice and mercy, and His love for children is clearly shown. In Matthew 19 we see Jesus's attitude toward children:

Then were there brought unto him little children, that he should put his hands on them, and pray: and the disciples rebuked them. But Jesus said, Suffer little children, and forbid them not, to come unto me: for of such is the kingdom of heaven. And he laid his hands on them, and departed thence. (Matt. 19:13-15)

God has told us that unrighteous people who have rejected Him and His son Jesus will ultimately be cast into the lake of fire with Satan and his angels who followed him. It is inconceivable that our God of justice would also cast these innocent children into that kind of eternal torment. While I am not a theologian, and scholars would certainly hold varying positions, my study of Scripture leads me to believe that God has the power to save these innocent children; and I trust that He will write their names in the Lamb's book of life unto eternal salvation.

Will I Be Reunited with My Departed Spouse in Heaven?

This is one of the most difficult questions to address because the answer which at first seems clear may not represent what we want to believe. There are verses which seem to indicate a negative answer, such as Matthew 22:30, which says, "For in the resurrection they neither marry, nor are given in marriage, but are as the angels of God in heaven." And Mark 12:25 has a similar answer, "For when they shall rise from the dead, they neither marry, nor are given in marriage; but are as the angels which are in heaven."

However, when examining the Greek text, the verb *gamousin* is only used to mean the act of marrying, as when a man takes a bride in marriage. Likewise, the verb *exgamizontai* means to give in marriage, as when the father gives his daughter to be married. So in a literal sense, this means that new marriages will not be conducted in heaven, since angels do not marry each other and neither will people marry in their resurrected bodies. However, I do not believe we can conclude that existing marriages will not be honored in the manner God chooses.

As usual, one needs to look at any verse or passage in actual context before accepting its presumed meaning. The passage from Matthew begins in 22:23 with a group of Sadducees (Jews who did not believe in resurrection) who were asking Jesus a trick question that they hoped would trip Him up. Their question was not really about marriage in heaven, but about resurrection. Jesus did not answer the stated question, but instead, answered the underlying agenda-driven question:

> Jesus answered and said unto them, Ye do err, not knowing the scriptures, nor the power of God. For in the resurrection they neither marry, nor are given in marriage, but are as the angels of God in heaven. But as touching the resurrection of the dead, have ye not read that which was spoken unto you by God, saying, I am the God of Abraham, and the God of Isaac, and the God of Jacob? God is not the God of the dead, but of the living. (Matt. 22:29-32)

Paul gives us an answer in 1 Thessalonians 4 which reassures us that we will see our departed loved ones who died as Christ-followers:

> But I would not have you to be ignorant, brethren, concerning them which are asleep, that ye sorrow not, even as others which have no hope. For if we believe that Jesus died and rose again, even so them also which sleep in Jesus will God bring with him. For this we say unto you by the word of the Lord, that we which are alive and remain unto the coming of the Lord shall not prevent them which are asleep. For the Lord himself shall descend from heaven with a shout, with the voice of the archangel, and with the trump of God: and the dead in Christ shall rise first: Then we which are alive and remain shall be caught up together with them in the clouds, to meet the Lord in the air: and so shall we ever be with the Lord. Wherefore comfort one another with these words. (1 Thess. 4:13-18)

Paul goes on to explain in 1 Corinthians 15 that our resurrected bodies will be completely different. He used the comparison of a plant which grows from a seed which must first be sown in the earth. The plant only comes to life after its seed is buried, and its form is different from that which was sown.

God has defined the kind of plant which will arise from its seed. Different kinds of seeds give rise to specific bodies, according to its kind.

There are heavenly bodies and earthly bodies, as God ordained in His created order. Both kinds of bodies are glorious in His eyes, yet there is a difference between the earthly and heavenly.

> So also is the resurrection of the dead. It is sown in corruption; it is raised in incorruption: It is sown in dishonour; it is raised in glory: it is sown in weakness; it is raised in power: It is sown a natural body; it is raised a spiritual body. There is a natural body, and there is a spiritual body. (1 Cor. 15:42-44)

We were born in the image of Adam, in earthly physical bodies, and will be raised in heavenly spiritual bodies. Because physical bodies cannot inherit the kingdom of God, our perishable bodies must be raised as imperishable bodies, in order to have eternal life. We will all be changed from mortal beings to immortal beings. This will be the fulfillment of the promise:

> Death is swallowed up in victory. O death, where is thy sting? O grave, where is thy victory? The sting of death is sin; and the strength of sin is the law. But thanks be to God, which giveth us the victory through our Lord Jesus Christ. (1 Cor. 15:54-57)

Therefore, we can be encouraged knowing that we will see our loved ones who have died in Christ as well as those who are still alive at the Rapture. The difference will be that we will all have resurrection bodies which are different from our current earthly bodies. Because our resurrected bodies will be both physical and spiritual, the love we have for our spouse (or spouses, in cases of remarried, widowed people) will be the kind of love which transcends emotional and physical love. Whether we will ultimately live together in heaven is not addressed, but we know that our joy and contentment will be complete, since there will be no sadness, pain, or suffering, as Revelation 21:4 states: "And God shall wipe away all tears from their eyes; and there shall be no more death, neither sorrow, nor crying, neither shall there be any more pain: for the former things are passed away."

For those of us whose spouses have also been saved, it is difficult to imagine spending eternity separated from them and not experiencing tears, sorrow, crying, and pain. However, we can have confidence in the wisdom and power of God to provide a joyful solution.

MY JOURNEY

The sudden death of my wife was, and continues to be, a source of grief and pain. It is not because I had any doubt whether her spirit would forever be in the presence of our Lord Jesus Christ. I trusted that this would be true, which comforted me for her sake. As the apostle Paul said in Philippians 1:21, "For to me to live is Christ, and to die is gain."

As comforting as that knowledge was, my personal sadness and grieving continued. But every time I found myself dwelling on my own sorrow, I would shift my focus to imagine the joy her spirit was experiencing. Without a sense of certainty about the exact nature of her afterlife status, my trust in God's promised salvation has sustained me during the healing process. I then learned that grieving was not only normal but necessary for my emotional health. The heartbreak and tears eventually gave way to a quiet confidence based on knowledge found in God's Word. Sadness at the loss of a loved one is better expressed than held inside. Even Jesus wept when He was told that His dear friend Lazarus had died.

Throughout my Christian life I had been led to believe that when we die our spirit goes immediately to heaven. The depth of my Bible studies over the past ten years had raised questions in my mind about this idea, but I had not taken the time and energy to test this assumption. I found myself unable to experience complete closure surrounding my wife's departure until

I could determine with as much certainty as possible where her soul and spirit had gone. Surely the answer could be found in the Bible, so I decided to search Scripture to find what God had revealed about life after death and then organize and record this information in book form, with the hope that readers would find it informative and engaging.

This exercise has been simultaneously challenging and rewarding. It has been challenging because there is no single chapter or book in the Bible that lays out a picture of the afterlife concisely and completely. Thankfully, I had access to several powerful Bible search tools which reduced the research effort to a more manageable task. My reward has been that my questions have been answered to my satisfaction and I trust that my readers will feel rewarded and enlightened as well.

We have explored at some length the details revealed in God's Word regarding our journey after we die. I thought it would be helpful to summarize the key elements, highlighting the signposts along the way:

- Upon the death of the body, the soul and spirit of the believer in Jesus Christ depart the body and proceed to paradise (not to be equated to heaven).

- The soul and spirit of those who rejected belief in Jesus will descend into Hades and await a future final judgment.

- At an undisclosed future time, Jesus will descend from heaven and take a position in the air above the earth. He will command all those Christians in paradise to ascend to join Him in the air, and He will snatch up (rapture) all believers still living to be gathered together with those who were called out of paradise.

- The entire group of believers will receive new bodies suitable for life in the heavenly realm and will follow Jesus to heaven.

- Then all these believers will stand before the judgment seat of

Jesus and receive rewards commensurate with their good works (or lack thereof) while they lived on earth. There is no condemnation since all have been granted salvation to eternal life in Christ.

- After this, God will turn His attention back to the Jewish people who continue to reject Jesus as Messiah. There will be seven years of Tribulation and pouring out of God's wrath upon the nation of Israel.

- After the end of this Great Tribulation, God will send Jesus to descend to Jerusalem with the armies of heaven and destroy His enemies in the battle referred to as the battle of Armageddon. At this Second Coming He will establish His kingdom on earth and restore the throne of David to Israel for a thousand years (the Millennium).

- During the Millennium, Satan will be bound in the bottomless pit and be unable to deceive those living on earth. At the end of Christ's thousand-year reign, Satan will be released for a short time to resume his efforts to draw people away from Jesus.

- God will then destroy all who follow Satan and cast them into the lake of fire, including Satan himself.

- God will then call forth all occupants of Hades to face the Great White Throne judgment. All those whose names are not found in the Lamb's book of life will be cast into the lake of fire, along with death and Hades, which will cease to exist.

- The eternal population of heaven will include those who were participants in the Rapture (Christ followers) and Jews who are admitted into Jesus' millennial kingdom.

- Next God will replace the existing earth and the heavens with a new heaven and a new earth. The center of the new earth will be the New Jerusalem. There will be no temple there, since God the Father and Jesus are themselves the temple. There are no longer any distinctions between Jews and Gentiles.

- There will be no night, only daylight, and neither will there be any sun. God will dwell there with His people and will be the source of the light, just as He was in the beginning of creation.

We can see that there are two different pathways to eternity. One path leads to an eternal life of peace and joy with God the Father and Jesus Christ in New Jerusalem. The other leads to eternal torment in the lake of fire. The ability to choose the better alternative was granted to all when Jesus suffered and died for the forgiveness of the sins of everyone. The only requirement is that one accept His gift of salvation by placing one's faith and trust in Him. Simply proclaim in your heart that you believe He is your personal savior and that you are saved by faith and not by anything you do in an effort to gain His favor. Jesus stated clearly, "For God so loved the world, that he gave his only begotten Son, that whosoever believeth in him should not perish, but have everlasting life." (John 3:16)

I sincerely hope that all who read this will embrace this blessed hope and encourage others who may be uncertain about the reason we should all have for the hope God has promised to us.

Further Study

Surely there are more questions to be answered regarding the afterlife. There are things we want to know and relationships we long to renew with departed family, friends, and loved ones. In writing this book, I have been drawn more deeply into God's Word than ever before. Even though it is written that no one can know all of His works from beginning to end, He has given us a wealth of information. We can know for certain that our ultimate home will be in the holy city with our heavenly Father and our Lord Jesus. We will gain more understanding if we are diligent in studying His Word and correctly interpreting and applying it.

There are many false assumptions which have shaped the beliefs of Christians and non-Christians alike. Only by careful study beyond simply reading our Bible can we replace misinterpretation and misapplication with real truth and understanding of the nature and character of God. May we follow these instructions always:

2 Timothy 2:15 – "Study to shew thyself approved unto God, a workman that needeth not to be ashamed, rightly dividing the word of truth."

John 8:31-32 – "If ye continue in my word, then are ye my disciples indeed; And ye shall know the truth, and the truth shall make you free."

Amen.

Dispensational Publishing House is striving to become the go-to source for Bible-based materials from the dispensational perspective.

Our goal is to provide high-quality doctrinal and worldview resources that make dispensational theology accessible to people at all levels of understanding.

Visit our blog regularly to read informative articles from both known and new writers.

And please let us know how we can better serve you.

Dispensational Publishing House, Inc.
PO Box 3181
Taos, NM 87571

Call us toll free 844-321-4202

www.DispensationalPublishing.com

CPSIA information can be obtained
at www.ICGtesting.com
Printed in the USA
FFHW010945040219
50393576-55542FF